Hey God

Authentic Prayers for Everyday Life and Journal

Volume 3

Solomon Jordan

Unless otherwise indicated, all Scripture references are taken from the King James Version of the Bible.

Contents

Personal Prayers   4

A Prayer for Salvation   5

A Prayer for When You Feel Far Away from God   6

A Prayer for Faith   7

A Prayer to Repent   8

A Prayer to Forgive Yourself   9

A Prayer to Walk in Purpose   10

PURPOSE ACTIVITY   11

A Prayer to Get Closer to God   14

A Prayer to Say Thank You   15

A Prayer for Your Friends   18

A Prayer for Protection   19

A Prayer to Start Your Day   20

A Prayer to End Your Day   21

A Prayer to Start Your Week   22

A Prayer to Start Your Month   23

A Prayer to End the Year   24

A Prayer to Begin the Year   25

A Prayer for Alignment with God   26

A Prayer for God's Timing   27

A Prayer to Fight Doubt   28

A Prayer for God's Correction   29

A Prayer for When It's Your Birthday   30

A Prayer for When You Face Disappointment   31

A Prayer to Hear God's Voice   32

A Prayer for Your Finances 33

Relationship Prayers 34

A Prayer for Your Marriage 35

A Prayer to Fight for Your Relationship 36

A Prayer after an Argument 37

A Prayer for Your Anniversary 38

A Prayer for Clarity in a Relationship 39

The Love Prayer 40

A Prayer to Love Again 41

A Prayer for Your Dating Relationship 42

A Prayer for Your Children 43

A Prayer for Your Heart 44

A Prayer Before You Go on a Date 45

A Prayer for When You're Single 46

A Prayer for When You Lose a Friend 47

A Prayer after a Breakup 48

A Prayer for Healthy Relationships 49

A Prayer for Your Future Spouse 50

A Prayer for When You Miss Them 51

Purpose Prayers 52

A Prayer to Not Settle 53

A Prayer for When You Need to Make a Tough Decision 54

A Prayer for Direction in Life 55

A Prayer for the Dream God Gave You 56

A Prayer to Overcome the Obstacles in Your Life 57

A Prayer to Bounce Back 58

A Prayer for When You Need God to Make a Way in a Situation 59

A Prayer to See People Clearly 60

A Prayer for God to Prepare You for the Opportunities Ahead   61

A Prayer for Favor and Open Doors   62

A Prayer Before You Go to Work   63

A Prayer to Not be Led by Your Feelings   64

A Prayer to Develop the Gifts that God Gave You   65

A Prayer to Keep Going   66

A Prayer to Grow   67

A Prayer for God to Open and Close Doors in Your Life   68

A Prayer to Embrace the Process   69

A Prayer to Take Accountability   70

Mental Health Prayers   71

A Prayer to Calm Your Mind   72

A Prayer for the Times You Feel Anxious   73

A Prayer to Help Fight Depression   74

A Prayer for When You've Outgrown Old Places   75

A Prayer to Keep the Vision God Gave You   76

A Prayer for When You're Disappointed   77

A Prayer to Fight Imposter Syndrome   78

A Prayer for When You Learn that Words Do Hurt   79

A Prayer to Help Fight Your Insecurities   80

A Prayer for the Times You Feel Overwhelmed   81

A Prayer When You're Emotionally Drained   82

A Prayer to Get Out of Your Own Head   83

Heart Prayers   84

A Prayer to Not Fall in Lust   85

A Prayer for Your Heart   86

A Prayer to Let Go and Grow   87

A Prayer for Your New Normal   88

A Prayer for When the Mind Replays What the Heart Can't Forget   89

A Prayer for the Silent Battles   90

A Prayer to Forgive   91

A Prayer for When You Face Rejection   92

A Prayer to Rest   93

A Prayer to Encourage Yourself   94

A Prayer to Believe Again   95

A Prayer to Make Peace with Your Past   96

A Prayer for When Your Feelings Are Hurt   97

A Prayer for When You're Triggered   98

A Prayer for When Your Heart Is Grieving   99

A Prayer for When You're Tempted to Quit   100

A Prayer for When You're Worried about Something   101

A Prayer for When You're Angry   102

A Prayer for Boundaries in A Relationship   103

A Prayer for When You Make A Mistake   104

A Prayer for When You Feel Lonely   105

A Prayer for Closure   106

A Prayer for Overthinking   107

A Prayer to Fight an Addiction   108

A Prayer for the Times You Feel Petty   109

A Prayer for When A Lot is Going On   110

A Prayer of Acceptance   111

A Prayer to Move On   112

A Prayer to Declutter Your Heart   113

A Prayer for When You're Tired   114

A Prayer to Feel Again   115

A Prayer for Family Wounds   116

A Prayer for Healing from the Trauma of Sexual   117

Prayers for Life   118

A Prayer to Trust God with what You Can't Control   119

A Prayer to Try Again   120

A Prayer for Someone Who Is Sick   121

A Prayer for When You're Trying to Have Children   122

A Prayer for When You've Been Hurt by People in Church   123

A Prayer When You're Breaking Generational Cycles   124

A Prayer for Patience   125

A Prayer for the In-between Seasons of Life   126

A Prayer for a Good Hair Day   127

A Prayer for God's Provision   128

A Prayer for When Someone Passes Away   129

A Prayer Before an Interview   130

A Prayer Before a Test   131

A Prayer to Resist Temptation   132

A Prayer for When You're Trying to Lose Weight   133

A Prayer for Healing   134

A Prayer for The First Day of a New Season   135

A Prayer for When It's Hard to Get out of Bed   136

A Prayer for When You Have a Bad Day   137

A Prayer While You Wait on God   138

A Prayer to Unlearn What No Longer Serves You   139

A Prayer to Not Become Attached to Things Not For You   140

A Prayer for Restoration   141

A Prayer to Pivot   142

A Prayer Before You Have a Tough Conversation   143

EASTER Day Prayer   144

Christmas Day Prayer   145

Mother's Day Prayer   146

A Prayer for Fathers   147

Affirmations   148

Affirmations to Start Your Day   149

Nighttime Affirmations   150

Growth Prayers   151

Faith Prayers   152

Heart Prayers   154

Relationship Prayers   155

Life Prayers   156

Hey God Journal   158

Hey,

I don't know where you are personally in your life right now. I don't know if this is your first time reading a "Hey God" book of you have purchased each one. Maybe everything is wonderful, and you are living out your wildest dreams. Maybe you are doing everything you can to survive, and your tears outnumber your laughs and you're just doing everything you can to hang on. No matter where you are, I have been there.

In every season of my life, prayer has been the constant that has kept me close to God. In First Thessalonians 5:17, the Apostle Paul instructs us to pray without ceasing. In other words, be in constant communication with God because communication is said to be the air to a relationship. It breathes life into a relationship and allows it to grow. Well, God and I have talked about a lot over my lifetime, and I wanted to provide you with a guide to help you in the moments where it's hard to find the right words to say. The times when you may ask, "Is God even listening?". My life is a testimony that not only is He listening but that he speaks, leads, guides, protects and above all else, He loves us through it all.

Please know that I am praying for you and believe that you will walk into all the things that you and God talk about. I pray that you grow in your relationship with Him and that when people see you, they don't see you, but they see God shining through you. – Solo

My Prayer for whoever reads this book: God, I pray for every person who reads the prayers in this book. May it connect their hearts to Yours. May it give them the strength to walk their journey, the wisdom for important and tough decisions, and guidance as they walk with You to the places that you both talk about.

In Jesus' name,

Amen.

To Those Who Made This Possible:

Thank You God

Thank You Kirsten

Thank You Mom and Dad

Thank You Brothers

Thank You Pastors and Mentors

Thank You Pain and Heart Break

Thank You Healing

Thank You Friends

And Thank You to everyone who supported the first and second edition of the "Hey God" Prayer book.

Your support has made this possible.

Personal Prayers

A Prayer for Salvation

Jesus, I have decided in my heart to follow You and become one of Your disciples. I believe that You are the Son of God and that you came to offer salvation. I believe that You died on the cross and rose again. You knew everything about me and still chose me. I believe You sacrificed Your life for me and love me. I trust You to lead and guide me through Your Word, The Holy Spirit and other disciples. I commit my life to You and pray that You have Your way in my life. May You increase, and may I decrease. I pray that when people see me, they do not see me at all, but instead see You shining through. Thank You.

In Jesus' name,

Amen.

A Prayer for When You Feel Far Away from God

Hey God,

I know You said that You would never leave or forsake me, but if I'm honest, I feel far away from You right now. A lot has been going on, and it feels like life is killing me. It's as if every time I try to look for You, it gets harder to see You through the chaos of my heart. I'm trying to quiet my feelings and allow my faith to lead me, but that's easier said than done. Help me to see You in the middle of everything going on right now. I know the best place to be is close to You. I let go of anything or anyone pulling me away from You. Help me to see You amid the storm, and I will walk towards You. I will not let the presence of a storm make me question if You're absent. I trust You, and I know that You are with me.In Jesus' name,

Amen.

A Prayer for Faith

Hey God,

I was thinking about what You placed in my heart to do, and I know I need You now more than ever to accomplish my calling. Faith is believing in things not yet seen but things that I desperately hope for. Develop the faith to walk on what seems impossible, for I know that all things are possible with You. I know You call me to walk on the impossible, destroy giants, pick up my cross, and love people back to life in You. So, if You called me to it, then You will see me through it. I pray that I see myself the way that You see me. You be God, and I will be obedient. I will not allow my doubt to outwork my faith, but I will use my rock of obedience and slingshot of worship to accomplish all You have placed in my heart.In Jesus' name,

Amen.

A Prayer to Repent

Hey God,

You saw what happened, and I'm sorry. I messed up. I allowed my emotions to lead me, and I reacted and made a decision that I need to make right. I refuse to allow my decisions to create a life that is in constant chaos, and I refuse to confuse condemnation with conviction. I know that my life is a result of my decisions and I want what You have for me. I will listen to Your voice as I apologize to anyone I might have hurt. I will learn and do what I need to so that this does not happen again. Thank You for guiding me through this and for loving me and not letting go.

In Jesus' name,

Amen.

A Prayer to Forgive Yourself

Hey God,

I have made some mistakes and haven't always gotten things right. Sometimes, my mistakes haunt me and block my view of the future. I've realized that everything that happened to me in life wasn't an attack from the enemy. Sometimes, I was the problem. Sometimes, I was the one in the wrong. I cursed them out and was led by my emotions to a place called regret. I know You said that You can make all things new. Can You help me to see myself through Your eyes and not my mistakes? Please help me learn from my mistakes, grow from my failures, and correct behaviors that don't serve me. Please help me to forgive myself and not confuse conviction with condemnation. I made a mistake, but I am not a mistake.

In Jesus' name,

Amen.

Isaiah 43:18-19 - Forget the former things; do not dwell on the past. See, I am doing a new thing! Now it springs up; do you not perceive it? I am making a way in the wilderness and streams in the wasteland.

A Prayer to Walk in Purpose

Hey God,

Please guide my heart in this journey of life. I know You created me for a purpose, and I don't want to chase the acceptance of people at the expense of missing You. I want what You have for me. If it is not from You, I don't want it. Help me use my gifts to build the dream You have placed in my heart. Please introduce me to me and help me to find the purpose of each season of my life. I know the plans that You have for me are good, but I also know they will require every part of me. And because of that, I lean my life into Your hands. You be God, and I will be obedient, and I will meet You at the places we talk about.

In Jesus' name,

Amen.

PURPOSE ACTIVITY

Discovering your purpose is a never-ending journey. Once you know your "why," you can focus on your what. I know what it is like to be confused about your purpose. My mentor helped me break down my purpose frustration by thinking through the following:

- Passion is what we want to do.

- Talent is what we can do.

- Purpose is what we are created to do.

As I began to list my thoughts on purpose through that filter, I began to ask the following questions:

1. What makes me feel alive in this season of my life? What activities or accomplishments bring me immense joy, fulfillment, or a sense of being?

_____

_____

_____

_____

_____

_____

2. What are my passions?

_____

_____

_____

_____

_____

_____

3. What are my strengths and talents?

_____
_____
_____
_____
_____
_____

4. What impact can I make in this season of my life?

_____
_____
_____
_____
_____
_____

5. What does success look like in this season of my life?

_____
_____
_____
_____
_____
_____

6. What did I pray for or about? Does God have me in this place for a reason?

_____
_____
_____
_____
_____
_____

Take these questions and answer them below. Use your answers as a guide to answer this question: **What problems ignite my passion, brings me fulfillment, and are easily handled by my strengths, ideas, and approach?**

A Prayer to Get Closer to God

Hey God,

Please keep me close to You. So many voices are trying to tell me who and what to be and do in this life. Please remove anything or anyone that pulls me away from You and add anything or anyone that pushes me closer to You. Please help me not allow the disappointments of my life to poison my faith. Help me to build the discipline to reject the trap of temptation. I want to be where You are. I want to see life from Your point of view and not my pain, trauma, or fears. Please don't allow me to confuse singing a worship song with living a life full of worship. I pray that I get to a place where when people see me, they see Your heart shining through me.

In Jesus' name,

Amen.

Psalm 27:4 One thing I ask from the Lord, this only do I seek: that I may dwell in the house of the Lord all the days of my life, to gaze on the beauty of the Lord and to seek him in his temple.

A Prayer to Say Thank You

Hey God,

I just want to say Thank You. You have always been there. When people left me, You stayed. When others gossiped about me, You spoke truth to my heart. When I was confused, You gave wisdom. You protected me, even from myself at times. You ended relationships and birthed new ones. You opened doors that needed to be opened and closed doors that needed to be closed. I see that man's rejection is your protection. You corrected me and ensured that I became more like You and not what happened to me. I can never repay You, but I can give You my life. My goal is to show You my appreciation through how I live my life. And when others see me, I pray they see Your heart shining through.

In Jesus' name,

Amen.

God I Want to Thank You for the Following:

1. _____
_____

2. _____
_____

3. _____
_____

4. _____
_____

5. _____
_____

6. _____
_____

7. _____
_____

8. _____
_____

9. _____
_____

10. _____
_____

11. _____
_____

12. _____
_____

13. _____
    _____

14. _____
    _____

15. _____
    _____

16. _____
    _____

17. _____
    _____

18. _____
    _____

19. _____
    _____

20. _____
    _____

A Prayer for Your Friends

Hey God,

Thank You for my friends. They are pretty awesome. You say that iron sharpens iron and that a friend loves at all times. I thank You that our friendship continues to push each other closer to You. May we not allow the cancer of drama to kill our relationship. I pray we always support and correct each other. May our friendship breathe life into our hearts, and when people see us, I pray they see You. I pray we always celebrate the wins and cover the losses of life. I pray that our friendship grows healthier over time. Guide us on how to handle conflict and not allow pride or pettiness to ruin a good thing. May I help them accomplish what You have called them to do. Help me to see my friends through Your eyes, and may we push each other to stand before You and hear "well done."

In Jesus' name,

Amen.

A Prayer for Protection

Hey God,

I pray for Your protection. You are my stronghold and my fortress, and it is in You that I trust. It's easy to allow fear to creep in, but You have not given me the spirit of fear. You have given me a spirit of power, love, and a sound mind. You remind me that no weapon formed against me shall prosper. Though they will form, they will not win. I pray that You give me the wisdom to avoid situations, people, and traps meant to harm me. I have peace knowing that no matter what comes, You are with me. So, I will not fear but trust that You watch over me.

In Jesus' name,

Amen.

A Prayer to Start Your Day

Hey God,

Have Your way in my life today.

I trust You more than anything else. I pray that today I will become more like You. I will walk in love and step over drama. I will walk by faith and not stumble over worry because I know You will work everything out. Help me to be the answer to someone's prayer today, and when people see me, I hope that they see Your heart shining through me. The goal is to leave everyone I encounter better than I found them and allow them to taste the fruit of the Spirit from our interaction. Please give me the wisdom and strength to handle anything that might come my way. I will not be led by my emotions today but by Your Spirit. I know that You are with me, and I trust You. So, I will continue to walk to the places that You have prepared for me today.

In Jesus' name,

Amen.

A Prayer to End Your Day

Hey God,

Thank You for walking with me and keeping me today. There were some good moments and not-so-good moments today. I'm doing my best not to let my thoughts run a marathon through my heart as I replay everything. I rest in the fact that with You, everything will work out. So, tonight, as I lie down, please give me Your peace that quiets the thoughts of my heart and allow me to rest in knowing that my future with You is more than I could ever imagine. Tomorrow is a new day filled with new promises. And we will keep walking to the places that we talk about.

In Jesus' name,

Amen.

A Prayer to Start Your Week

Hey God,

Please guide my heart this week and help me grow closer to You. May I use my gifts to build the things You placed in my heart. You have permission to do whatever You need to do in my life. Add and remove whoever or whatever You need to in my life. I don't want to fall into the trap of distraction or comparison this week. Please continue to heal my heart to the point that my triggers become my testimonies. I can't let what happened to me determine how I show up in life. May love be the theme of my life, and Your joy be my strength. May I leave everyone I encounter this week better than I found them. I know that not everything that happens to me is good, but I trust You to work everything out for my good and Your glory.

In Jesus' name,

Amen.

A Prayer to Start Your Month

Hey God,

As I start this month, I pray that You continue to guide my heart. A lot has happened these past few months. There have been some beautiful moments and some challenging moments. People came, and people left; some things went right, and some things went left, but You have helped me through it all. Continue to lead me as I release what was lost, and I walk by faith to the places that You and I talk about. May I use my gift to continue to build the vision that You have given me. Please help me to be present and enjoy the beautiful moments this month. May I not allow the feeling of being behind make me abandon the plans that You have for me. If I'm ever going in the wrong direction this month, please correct me. This month is another opportunity to love others, build the vision, make memories, and grow closer to You. And I will use it as such.

In Jesus' name,

Amen.

A Prayer to End the Year

Hey God,

Thank you for seeing me through another year. This year has really tested my faith, mental health, finances, and heart. Yet, through it all, I'm still standing. There were some good and bad days. But I'm still here and standing with the dream You gave me! I'm thankful that You helped me grow through some tough moments and didn't allow them to overcome me. As I prepare for next year, I release and forgive any hurt and pain from this past year. I celebrate the mountains we have climbed and the victories we have won. Thank You for the new relationships, as well as those that ended. I've learned that not everything that happens to me is good, but I've seen you turn any situation around for good and Your Glory. So, as I enter this new year, I pick my cross and follow you to the places we talk about.

In Jesus's name,

Amen.

A Prayer to Begin the Year

Hey God,

Please guide my heart this year.

I want to walk in purpose, not in comparison, doubt, or misalignment. I know that You will call me to do hard things this year, but with You, they are not impossible. Give me the strength to do something that may hurt my heart in the moment but bring me closer to You in the future. I can't grow if I never face the giants in my life. So, I will put my rock of obedience in my slingshot of worship and conquer the giants on the path to where You've called me to be. I will listen for Your voice in every situation. Guide my heart to the right relationships and away from traps and distractions. Correct me if I'm off track, and give me rest when I'm tired. Give me Your strength when I'm weak and Your peace when I'm worried. At the end of this year, may I be closer to the places we talk about as I keep my eyes on You.

In Jesus' Name,

Amen.

A Prayer for Alignment with God

Sometimes, we want something or someone to work out so badly that we convince ourselves it must be from God. Then, when it doesn't work out, we question God. Our feelings are indicators, but they are horrible leaders. I have learned that what I want and what God wants for me can be very different at times. I have wanted to end certain things that God wanted me to continue, and I have wanted to continue things that God wanted me to end. I have learned that the best place to be is in alignment with God, and I want what He wants for me. Not everything or everyone will be perfect for me, but with God, it will all serve a purpose for me.

Prayer: God, have Your way in my life. Please remove or add who or what You need to in my life. Lead, prepare, and correct me so I can walk into the places we talk about. I trust You, for I know that You are guiding me to the places that we talk about. So, You be God, and I will be obedient as I walk in alignment with you.

In Jesus' Name

Amen.

A Prayer for God's Timing

Hey God,

Do whatever You need to do in my life so that I arrive at the places that we talk about at the right time. Guide me, correct me, and lead me. Heal my heart so that I don't arrive at those places heartless, and build my character so that I can remain in those places. Remove and add whoever You need to in my life. Please open every door in my life that needs to be opened, and please close any door that needs to be closed. I will not allow the feeling of being behind make me abandon the plans You have for me. You be God, and I'll be obedient and trust Your timing.

In Jesus' Name,

Amen.

A Prayer to Fight Doubt

Hey God,

I'm looking at what's in front of me, and my faith and doubt are at war for my heart. I've learned that it's not the voice I hear that determines where I end up, but the voice that I believe that determines my path. I can't allow my doubt to talk me out of my faith. I choose to believe Your voice over any doubt. Help me to see myself the way You see me. With You, it doesn't matter what's in front of me because You make the impossible possible. You don't even need a fight to be fair in order to win it; You just need my obedience.

In Jesus' Name,

Amen.

A Prayer for God's Correction

Hey God,

I don't want to be in the same place this time next year. Introduce me to me. Help me to see myself the way that You see me. Do whatever You need to do in my life that pushes me closer to You. Heal my heart so that my triggers become my testimonies. Add or remove whoever or whatever You need to. Develop in me the character to not just reach the places that we talk about, but the character to remain in the places and relationships that we talk about. You have permission to do whatever is needed in my life, for Your correction is for my protection.

In Jesus's name

Amen

A Prayer for When It's Your Birthday

Hey God,

Today is my birthday. Thank You for guiding me through another year. A lot has happened since my last birthday. Thank You for the moments that made me laugh from my soul, and thank You for holding me when my tears came from my soul. I saw You open doors that only You could open for me. I've had some situations that made me understand the scripture "Jesus Wept ."As I enter into the new year, I have one request. I want to walk with you closer than I ever have before. I pray that I continue to grow closer to You this next year and walk in purpose and not comparison. Help me overcome any obstacle in my path. Continue to teach me how to love people and place people in my life who You have taught how to love. My goal this year is that when people see me, they don't see me, but they see You shining through. Correct me, guide me, and teach me to steward the things You have blessed me with. This year, I will grow in discipline and purpose. You be God, and I will be obedient and keep walking to the places that we talk about.

In Jesus' name

Amen

A Prayer for When You Face Disappointment

Hey God,

So it didn't work out. I prayed, worked hard, had faith, and believed…….but it didn't work out. I began to ask myself, did I do something wrong? But You reminded me that You are in control, and rejection is for my protection. I either didn't need it, or I was not ready for it, and maybe it wasn't my time yet. Either way, I have learned that I can't walk by faith carrying the disappointments of life. The right thing at the wrong time is a recipe for frustration. I choose to trust You even when I don't understand. I choose to still get out of the boat and walk. Thank You for always looking out for me. I trust You to work out my life for good and Your glory.

In Jesus's name

Amen.

A Prayer to Hear God's Voice

Hey God,

May Your voice be louder than everything else in my heart. I want to be led by You and not my emotions, opinions, or culture. Open the eyes of my heart to see You speaking to me through people and situations. May Your words guide me when I'm lost. Remove anything that distracts my heart from Your voice. If it's not from You, then I don't want it or need it. You be God, and I'll be obedient as I follow Your voice to the places that we talk about.

In Jesus's name

Amen

A Prayer for Your Finances

Hey God,

Please teach me how to be a good steward of my finances. I don't want to use my faith for a miracle because of a lack of discipline. I know that money does not fix all of my problems but I know that not stewarding my finances will add to my problems. Please help me use the gifts You gave me to grow my finances. Develop the character and the discipline not to consume what I should be saving and investing. Allow me to become an answer to the financial needs of those I encounter. Help me to live a life filled with true riches. A life that is filled with joy, love, and peace. I don't want to chase money my entire life. I want to use money to build a life that allows me to continue walking to the places we talk about.

In Jesus's name

Amen

Relationship Prayers

A Prayer for Your Marriage

Hey God,

Our goal is to build a marriage that honors You in every way. We want people to see You and Your love when they look at our marriage. In this marriage, we will be led by Your Spirit and not our emotions, and love will be the foundation upon which we build. We will forgive when we get hurt and work through issues in a way that honors You. We will protect this union from anything that looks to tear it apart. Please help us to see each other through your eyes and not our pain, trauma, past, or insecurities. Surround us with friends who speak life into us and strengthen our union. May we support each other in the calling You have for each of us, and may we be a safe place where the heart of our spouse can reside. We will encourage each other to live the gospel and walk in love. May our marriage fill us with life. Our goal is to push each other to stand before You and hear You say, "Well done."

In Jesus' name,

Amen.

A Prayer to Fight for Your Relationship

Hey God,

This hurts like hell. I keep telling myself that, at some point, this has to get better. I'm really trying to make this relationship work, but it's hard. I know that I can't do this alone. You know my heart, and You know our history. Please don't allow me to throw away something that is hard in the moment but worth it in the end. Heal our hearts so that we can fight like love for this. Surround us with people to help us and remove anything bad for us. Teach us how to love each other. Nobody ever said love would be easy, but true love is worth the cost.

In Jesus' Name,

Amen.

A Prayer after an Argument

Hey God,

So, we just got into it, and I'm really upset right now. I don't want to be led by my emotions, but they are all that I can hear right now. Please help me to calm down. I don't want to argue, but I do want to find a resolution. Help me to approach this in a way that will lead to a resolution and not drama. Give me the words to say and help me communicate in a way that allows the conversation to move forward. If we need help to communicate, please bring the right people in to help us. Help me to produce the fruit of the Spirit and not the spirit of pettiness, drama or division.

In Jesus' Name,

Amen.

A Prayer for Your Anniversary

Hey God,

Thank You for this relationship. We have made it another year together. This year was filled with good and challenging moments, but through it all, we walked through it together. It wasn't a perfect year, but it was a testimony to the power of our love for each other. Please keep Your hand on us and help us always to see each other through Your eyes. May we honor You in the way that we love each other. Help us continue building a relationship where You can birth something beautiful. Help us work through the difficult moments so our relationship doesn't become hard. Please help us be safe spaces for each other that allow intimacy to grow. Please remove anything or anyone that would try to destroy what You've put together. May this next year be even better than the last, and may it be filled with love, healthy communication, beautiful memories, and You.

In Jesus' Name,

Amen.

A Prayer for Clarity in a Relationship

Hey God,

You see this relationship that I am in. Open the eyes of my heart and help me to see this relationship from Your point of view. Don't allow me to confuse loneliness or desperation with love. I don't want my need for love to make me fall in lust with a dream of what will never be. Help me to discern between the right and wrong person. You know the desires of my heart; so, please don't allow me to throw away a relationship that is hard in the moment but worth it in the end. I don't want my past experiences to ruin my future relationships. For I have learned that people can hurt you, but the right people can heal you.

In Jesus' Name,

Amen.

The Love Prayer

Hey God,

Please don't let my need for love allow me to confuse attention, lust, and chemistry with true love. Heal my heart because I can't walk in love with a broken heart. Please teach me how to love and receive love. Show me how to build a gate around my heart and not a wall. I don't want to arrive to relationships heartless because I will need my heart to walk in love. Do such a work in my heart that people know that I learned how to love from You.

In Jesus' Name,

Amen.

A Prayer to Love Again

Hey God,

If I'm honest, the thought of loving someone scares me, so much so that I've now built a wall around my heart that requires perfection to acquire it. I know I'm created to give and receive love, but the thought of letting someone in scares me. I know love hurts, but trauma destroys. Please heal my heart so I can walk in love again. I haven't yet met everyone who will love me in this life, and I don't want my view of them to be led by the pain of my past. Open the eyes of my heart and guide me in my relationships. Teach me how to love to the point that it's evident that I learned from You. I know people can hurt me, but I believe the right people can heal me. I refuse to allow the actions of one person to determine how I show up in the world. I will learn the lesson, set the boundary, and move forward in love and not pain.

In Jesus' Name,

Amen.

A Prayer for Your Dating Relationship

Hey God,

You see this relationship that I am in. Our goal is to build a relationship that honors each other but, more importantly, You. One that is healthy, filled with love, affection, and You. Open the eyes of our hearts and show us the right direction for this relationship. Help us develop healthy communication and boundaries that protect our hearts and allow us to build a healthy relationship. As we grow closer together, help us also grow closer to You. Help us to honor each other in this relationship and make decisions that won't haunt us if this relationship does not work out. I trust You to guide us and not allow us to settle for something that is not meant for us out of fear of being alone. Surround us with wise people who can speak life and wisdom into us. You have permission to correct us in any area, for your correction is our protection.

In Jesus' name,

Amen.

A Prayer for Your Children

Hey God,

Thank You for my children. Help me to be the best parent to my child and give me the strength to love them as You love us. I have learned truly what it means to love someone more than myself, and I know that I need your help to guide them through this life. May I raise them to know You and love others. Help me to impart wisdom as they experience life. Help me to see and develop the gifts that You have placed in them. May my life be an example to them as I walk with You. I will show them how to love, give, be strong, stand up for those who can't and speak for those who have no voice. I can't protect them from everything, but with you, I can prepare them. Keep Your hand on them as they go through life. Bless them with friends during every season of life that push them closer to You. Teach them how to guard their heart and not allow life to create a wall around it. Please correct them, guide them, and love them as only You can. I pray that I raise them in such a way that they hear, "Well done thou good and faithful servant."

In Jesus' name,

Amen.

A Prayer for Your Heart

Hey God,

Teach me how to guard my heart and not build a wall around it. I need my heart to walk in love, and I have learned that I can't love very well with a broken heart. I have been through some experiences that make it hard to trust people and believe their intentions are good. I can see the wall forming around my heart, and I can't allow those who hurt me to determine how I show up in future and present relationships. Help me to build a gate around my heart but not a wall. Help me to heal and learn who I should "know" in life and who I should say "no" to in life. Help me create healthy boundaries and not destructive habits. Heal the areas that hurt to talk about. I refuse to lose my heart, for it is the soil where my relationships grow.

In Jesus' name,

Amen.

A Prayer Before You Go on a Date

Hey God,

You see this person I'm about to go out with. May I see them through Your eyes. Don't allow me to confuse loneliness or desperation with potential love. Please help me to discern between the right person and the wrong person quickly. You know the desires of my heart, and I pray for guidance along the way. Help me to be led by love and not lust. I don't want to create a soul tie with a soul that is just passing by. Please help me not to allow past issues to ruin a good thing. In the end, the goal is to build a life filled with love and memories and push each other close to You. If I'm not ready or if this is toxic, end it now. You don't even have to explain.

In Jesus' name,

Amen.

A Prayer for When You're Single

Hey God,

Please help me to make this season of my life one of the best. You know the desires of my heart, and you know I desire to be in a relationship filled with love, life, and You. During this season, could you help me to see the beauty of life? May I not allow the anxiousness to be in a relationship to make me settle for something less than I deserve and make me miserable. Singleness is not a disease; it is an opportunity to bloom. In this season, introduce me to me. May I see the world through Your heart. May I know who I am and who You have called me to be. Teach me how to love myself so that I can know how to love others. Prune me to become healthy during this time to prepare me for a relationship when the time comes. And no matter what happens in my future, help me build a life full of love.

In Jesus' name,

Amen.

A Prayer for When You Lose a Friend

Hey God,

You saw what happened between me and _____. If I'm honest, this hurts. I know life is full of seasons, including relationships, and it seems that the season for this relationship has ended. Please help me to process this in a healthy way that allows me to move forward in life without the baggage of heartbreak. I know that I was created for friendship, and I don't want this situation to infect and destroy my view on friendship. I pray that I learn the lessons from this relationship and take the memories with me. I will miss them, but I pray that You keep Your hands on them. May You heal any parts of their heart that need to be healed, and may they know the beauty of friendship.

In Jesus' name,

Amen.

A Prayer after a Breakup

Hey God,

My heart is broken. I thought that would work out, but I can't see past my tears right now. I have moments when I think I'm strong, but then a memory hits me, and the uncertainty of, "will it ever work out for me" scares me. Even though I really wanted it to work, I have learned the definition of true love from You, and You showed me that I am worthy of love. I need You to heal my heart because I can't walk in love with a broken heart, and it hurts to love right now. I ask that You come in and make all things new as only You can. Heal my heart and give me the peace that quiets the thoughts and fears of my heart. This hurts, but I trust You to work all things out in my life. I know You can create a future so beautiful that it heals the pain of this moment.

In Jesus' name,

Amen.

A Prayer for Healthy Relationships

Hey God,

I know relationships take a lot of work, and I have experienced some amazing relationships and I've experienced some relationships that I still don't talk about. Please help me build healthy relationships that fill me with life and not drain the life out of me. Teach me how to give and receive love. Help me to guard my heart with boundaries so that I don't lose it to trauma. May my relationships be filled with love, accountability, joy, communication, and purpose. But most of all, may all of my relationships push us closer to You.

In Jesus's name

Amen

A Prayer for Your Future Spouse

Hey God,

You know my heart's desires, and I desire to be married. I know you're preparing me to not just fall in love, but to embody love. I pray that my next relationship is from You. I pray that as You are working on me, you are also working on my future spouse. I pray that you are healing any broken, damaged, or hidden areas of our hearts. We can't walk in love without our hearts. Please teach both of us how to love. Please help us to create boundaries in our lives now that protect our hearts from unnecessary lessons. Help us learn how to address issues in a healthy way so that our issues don't destroy us. I want a marriage filled with two people who love God and love each other.

In Jesus's name

Amen

A Prayer for When You Miss Them

Hey God,

I was doing okay, and then their memory snuck up on me. I remember the small things. The things that made me see past everything else. I'm not going to lie; the memories bring back all kinds of emotions. I thought goodbye would be like freedom, but it really feels lonely. Help me heal my heart so the memories don't trip me up. I know I'll need my heart when I cross paths with love in the future because I haven't met everyone who will love me in life yet. May I not confuse my feelings for faith and walk back to something I prayed my way out of.

In Jesus's name

Amen

Purpose Prayers

A Prayer to Not Settle

Hey God,

Don't allow me to settle for anything that is not for me. I don't want to walk in a life that doesn't fit me. Please open every door in my life that needs to be opened and close every door that needs to be closed. Remove and add whoever and whatever you need to in my life. Correct, guide, and speak to me. I don't want to settle for a hallucination of what You placed in my heart when I can walk in the dream that You gave me.

In Jesus's name,

Amen.

A Prayer for When You Need to Make a Tough Decision

Hey God,

You see this decision in front of me. It's the only thing I can think about. I'm torn, and I need to make the right decision. Help me to see this situation from Your point of view and give me the strength to make the right decision. Even if the right decision may hurt my heart in the moment, I know it will bring me peace in the future. I trust You. You be God, and I will be obedient.

In Jesus' name,

Amen.

A Prayer for Direction in Life

Hey God,

You see where I am in life, and You know where I need to be. I'm at a point where I don't want to waste time going in the wrong direction. I need to know where to go and when. I want to walk in purpose and not confusion. I have learned that my passion is what I want to do, my talent is what I can do, and my purpose is what I am supposed to do. I don't want an unhealthy passion to lead me away from my purpose, and I will not allow the wind and waves of life to make me stay in a sinking ship when You are calling me to walk on something that looks like it could drown me. I ask You to open every door that needs to be opened and close every door that needs to be closed in my life. I will listen to Your voice as I know You will guide me to the places that we talk about.

In Jesus' name,

Amen.

A Prayer for the Dream God Gave You

Hey God,

I have this dream in my heart that You gave me. It's what we talk about all the time. It seems that at times I have to walk through a nightmare to get to my dream, but I refuse to stop believing and building because of a dark night. Thank You for the gift of another opportunity to build with the gifts that You gave me. My goal is to build something that brings You glory. Give me the wisdom to know who and what to "know' and who and what to "No". Keep my heart pure so I don't reach the top without it. Give me the strength to push and rest at the right times. May Your voice be louder than the doubts in my head as I look for You any time I am lost. I know that all things are possible with You, even the dream You placed in my heart.

In Jesus' name,

Amen.

A Prayer to Overcome the Obstacles in Your Life

Hey God,

You see everything that is happening in my life. It's a lot, but I know that with You I will overcome everything that is coming against me. I will not be led by my emotions, but I will allow Your Spirit to guide me. I know that with You all things are possible, including this obstacle in front of me. So, I will not worry, but I will keep walking. I will pick up my rock of obedience and place it in my slingshot of worship to defeat the giants in my life. With You by my side, everything will work out. So, I will stop worrying about the outcome and trust you as I keep walking to the places that we talk about.

In Jesus' name,

Amen.

A Prayer to Bounce Back

Hey God,

I saw myself in the mirror, and it's time to get back up. I fell off and stayed down for a while. It felt like life was pressing down on me, and the more I struggled, the tighter life became. I won't lie, I became numb and comfortable in my valley, but now it's time to get back up. I know You're calling me higher, and I can't walk in purpose when I've dropped my calling. I've learned that You call me by my name and not what happened to me. I've also learned that faith and doubt speak to my heart at the same time, and whoever I choose to listen to will determine my path in life. I choose to believe faith. Please give me the strength to get back up and pick up my cross. I'm following Your lead and am coming back from what tried to kill me.

In Jesus' name,

Amen.

A Prayer for When You Need God to Make a Way in a Situation

Hey God,

You see this situation that I'm in. If I'm honest, it looks impossible from my point of view. You said that with You all things are possible, and I need You to make a way like only You can. I have done all that I know how to do, and now I stand on my faith, trusting You. I won't allow fear and worry to attack the faith of my heart. You're my foundation, and I know that no situation is too big for You. You've defeated giants, changed hearts, restored lives, AND conquered death. No matter what happens, I trust You to work everything out for my good and Your glory. You be God, and I will be obedient. I will walk by faith and not fear to the places that we talk about.

In Jesus' Name,

Amen.

A Prayer to See People Clearly

Hey God,

Open the eyes of my heart. Allow me to see clearly. Help me to learn where to place people in my heart. I want to see people through Your eyes and not my pain, trauma, fear, or false rumor. I don't want my future relationships to suffer because of the pain of my past relationships. Please heal the broken areas of my heart so that I can walk in love with people and not trip over the triggers from my past. Give me discernment so that I don't give everyone access to parts of me that only a few should have. Please help me build boundaries that protect me and not walls that isolate me. And when people see me, I pray they see Your heart shining through.

In Jesus' name,

Amen.

A Prayer for God to Prepare You for the Opportunities Ahead

Hey God,

Please prepare me for the things that we talk about. Develop my character so that I cannot only arrive at those places but remain there. Help me to not allow the feeling of being behind in my life, make me abandon the plans You have for me. When I see the opportunities in front of me, help me to see myself the way that You see me, so I don't talk myself out of them. I trust You. Please keep developing me until my opportunities become my testimonies.

In Jesus' name,

Amen.

A Prayer for Favor and Open Doors

Hey God,

I need You in this life. I ask that You keep Your hand on me as I follow You. Please open up every door in my life that needs to be opened and close every door that needs to be closed. Keep me humble by not allowing any win to go to my head or any loss to destroy my heart. I know that walking in Your favor will open doors that only You can open, and I want what You have for me. Guide my path and give me success as I honor You. At the end, I pray that I live a life that allows You to say, "Well done, good and faithful servant."

In Jesus' name,

Amen.

A Prayer Before You Go to Work

Hey God,

As I prepare to go to work today, I pray that You are with me. I know my life is in Your hands, so I will not worry. Please keep me from going off on petty or rude co-workers and customers. Help me to see them as You see them. Help me to keep Your vision as my guiding force and remind me that culture's dream can become the Christian's nightmare. Even though I walk through the valley of rude people, uncertainty, and frustration, I will fear no evil, for You are with me. Your Holy Spirit keeps me in the right mind, employed, and on the path to what we talk about. You are preparing my character through the test and trials of obedience in the presence of everyone. This produces my anointing, for I know that if I survive this job, I can survive anything. Surely, student loans will not follow me all the days of my life. For I will be excellent where You called me, and I will walk to the places we talk about and hear You say, "Well done, thou good and faithful servant."

In Jesus' name,

Amen.

A Prayer to Not be Led by Your Feelings

Hey God,

My emotions are trying to lead me, and I can't follow them. I have followed them before, and they led me to place called regret. I want to walk by faith and not by my emotions. My emotions are great indicators, but they are horrible leaders. Help me to not allow my feelings to talk me out of my faith. I will feel my emotions and work through them, but I will walk by faith to the places that we talk about.

In Jesus' name,

Amen.

A Prayer to Develop the Gifts that God Gave You

Hey God,

Don't allow me to waste anything that You have given me. Any gift from You is good, and I want to use my gifts to build the things that You have placed in my heart. Develop in me the character to maintain the opportunities and relationships that my gifts bring me into. Surround me with people and environments that will grow what You placed on the inside of me. Help me to not allow any failure go to my heart or any win to go to my head. And help me to see myself the way that You see me so that I don't talk myself out of anything that is for me. I'll develop my gifts and use them to build what we talk about.

In Jesus' name,

Amen.

A Prayer to Keep Going

Hey God,

I'm holding on to the word that You gave me. If I'm honest, it's hard right now, and I'm tired. Please don't let me settle in this place. I don't want to make a home in a place that was meant to be temporary. You call me to walk on what would normally drown me, and I can't confuse getting wet with drowning. Give me Your peace that quiets my doubts. Give me Your strength to keep walking, even when I'm unsure. Correct me and guide me. I don't want to settle for a hallucination of what You placed in my heart when I can walk in the dream that You gave me.

In Jesus' name,

Amen.

A Prayer to Grow

Hey God,

I don't want to be in the same place next year. Introduce me to me and help me see myself the way that You see me. Do whatever You need to do in my life that pushes me closer to You. Heal my heart so that my triggers become my testimonies. Add or remove whoever or whatever You need to in my life. Develop in me the character to not just reach the places that we talk about, but the character to remain in those places. You have permission to do whatever is needed in my life, for Your correction is my protection.

In Jesus' name,

Amen.

A Prayer for God to Open and Close Doors in Your Life

Hey God,

Please open up every door in my life that needs to be opened and close every door that needs to be closed. Please remove whoever You need to remove and add whoever You need to add. Correct me and guide me. If it's not from You, then I don't want it or need it. I don't want to confuse my faith with my impatience and rush into something not meant for me. I don't want to settle for a hallucination of what You placed in my heart when I can walk in the dream that You gave me. You be God, and I will be obedient and walk through the doors you open to the places that we talk about.

In Jesus' name

Amen.

A Prayer to Embrace the Process

Hey God,

Do whatever you need to do to develop me into the person I need to be to walk into the places that You have for me. Develop the character I need to not just arrive at the places we talk about but to remain in those places. I've learned that when I can't control what is happening in my life, then I have to control how I respond. I have survived everything that has tried to take me out. I don't understand why everything has happened to me the way it has in my life, but I trust that You will use it all for good and Your glory. Please do such a work in me that, when people see me, they see Your heart shining through.

In Jesus's name

Amen

A Prayer to Take Accountability

Hey God,

Please keep me accountable for the things that we talk about. We talk about some amazing things, and I know what You have for me is good. But I also know that faith without works is dead. Don't let me talk myself out of anything You've called me to. Develop in me the character to reach the places we talk about and remain in those places. Introduce me to me. Let me see myself through Your eyes. I don't want to be the reason the things we talk about don't happen. Surround me with people who push me towards purpose and place in environments that will grow me. I know that if You call me to something, then I know You will also see me through it as well.

In Jesus's name

Amen

Mental Health Prayers

A Prayer to Calm Your Mind

Hey God,

My thoughts are at war with my heart, and my mind is a battlefield. Give me Your peace to calm the thoughts of my heart. Give me the strength to accept what has happened, the wisdom on what to do next and the hope to know that with You all things work out for my good and Your glory. I don't want to confuse my desperation with my faith and create a mess. You never said that there wouldn't be storms, but Jesus did show me that no matter what is going on around us, we can find peace in the middle of the storm and walk on what is trying to drown us. So, I lay down my worries, and I pick up Your peace and rest in You.

In Jesus' name,

Amen.

A Prayer for the Times You Feel Anxious

Hey God,

Everything feels a little crazy right now. I'm trying my best not to be anxious, but You see the worries of my life crashing against the peace of my heart. Every time I try to pull myself up, another wave comes to push me back down. You told me to be anxious for nothing but to stay in prayer. I can't control everything happening right now, but I can trust You. I know that not everything that happens to me is good, but I believe You can turn any mess into a miracle. For You are where my hope comes from, and You will lead my heart through this valley of anxiety to the places we talk about.

In Jesus' name,

Amen.

A Prayer to Help Fight Depression

Hey God,

It feels like the weight of life is holding me down, and I can't move. My thoughts are running a marathon of worry and anxiety through my heart, and it's easier to just become numb because the pain of trying to feel is too much. You said that You would trade my ashes for beauty and that You would be an ever-present help during my times of need. Well, I need Your help to get through this. Help me to see past this fog of uncertainty and heal the parts of my heart that make it hard to hold on to hope. Open my heart to those You send to help me through this. I will continue stand on the promise that You work all things out. For I have learned that not everything that happens to me is good, but You can turn any situation around for my good and your glory.

In Jesus' name,

Amen.

A Prayer for When You've Outgrown Old Places

Hey God,

Recently, I've been frustrated. It seems like a lot of things don't fit me or my life anymore, and the more I have tried to make them fit, the more they have stretched me thin. I'm growing, and I've realized that what used to fill me up now leaves me wanting more. I'm not okay with trading my future by staying in what's familiar. I want what You have for me. Guide me to people, places and environments that will push me closer to You. Add whatever or whoever You need to in my life so that I develop into who You have called me to be. Give me the strength to walk away from what is not for me as I walk towards what You and I talk about.

In Jesus' name,

Amen.

A Prayer to Keep the Vision God Gave You

Hey God,

I've realized that not everyone can see the vision that You've placed in my heart. Everyone is telling me that it sounds crazy and that it doesn't make sence. But, I've learned that faith doesn't make sense, but it does make miracles. Please guide me to people who see me through Your eyes. Help me to not allow the doubt of others to make me doubt the vision that You gave me. Though people may not understand the vision, prevent my need to change it in order for them to accept it. The fruit of the vision will be proof that following You was the correct path, for people have opinions but You have dominion.

In Jesus' name,

Amen.

A Prayer for When You're Disappointed

Hey God,

So, it didn't work out. I prayed, worked, had faith, and did everything I knew how to do. Yet, it still didn't work out. I asked myself if I had done something wrong, but You reminded me that You are in control and just because it didn't work out, doesn't mean that it will never work out. I either didn't need it, wasn't ready for it, or it was not the right time. I have learned that I can't walk by faith carrying the disappointments of life. The right thing at the wrong time is a recipe for frustration. I choose to trust You even when it doesn't work out, and I don't understand. I choose to get out of the boat and walk on top of my disappointments to the places that we talk about. Thanks for looking out for me.

In Jesus' name,

Amen.

A Prayer to Fight Imposter Syndrome

Hey God,

There is a voice telling me that I don't belong here. And if I'm honest, there are times when I wonder if that is the thought of everyone else. I know that both faith and doubt will speak to my heart and whichever one I choose to believe will determine my path in life. I also know that if You call me to anything, You will see me through it as well. I'm not an imposter, but I am called and chosen for such a times as this. I will not confuse perfection with anointing, and I will not confuse humility with low self-thinking. I will stand in the places that You have called me to, confidently knowing that if You're for me, it doesn't matter who is against me.

In Jesus' name,

Amen.

A Prayer for When You Learn that Words Do Hurt

Hey God,

I have always heard, "Sticks and stones may break my bones, but words will never hurt me." Well, words do hurt, and there are certain conversations, text messages and words that have lasted longer than the relationships. There are times when I miss the relationship but remember the disrespect. Help me to not allow their words to replace Your words in my heart. I don't want to live a life that is focused on proving people wrong. I want to live the life that You have for me. People may have opinions, and but You have dominion. So, I release the pain of those words because I want to become better and not bitter. I will rest in Your words over my life.

In Jesus' name,

Amen.

A Prayer to Help Fight Your Insecurities

Hey God,

The voices in my head seem to be louder than the faith in my heart right now, and they keep telling me why it can't be me. Help me to see myself through Your eyes because it's hard to feel confident when I don't feel secure in who I am. I know You didn't give me a spirit of fear, for You call me to walk on what could drown me. I pray Your voice becomes louder than the doubts in my heart. For if You call me to it, You will guide me through it. I will not allow fear to determine my future, but I will keep walking to the places that we talk about. I will put my rock of obedience in my slingshot of worship and kill the giants in front of me.

In Jesus' name,

Amen.

A Prayer for the Times You Feel Overwhelmed

Hey God,

If I'm honest, life has become overwhelming. I am doing my best, but it seems like my heart is taking on worry and drowning in the sea of life. I need Your guidance right now. Help me to see life from Your point of view and not allow my view to overwhelm me. Show me what to pick up, what to put down and what to give to You. Please give me Your peace that quiets my worries and fears. I don't know how everything will work out, but I know that with You, everything will work out for my good and Your glory.

In Jesus' name,

Amen.

A Prayer When You're Emotionally Drained

Hey God,

My heart is tired. I'm trying to keep it all together, but it seems that the more I try to hold on to everything, the heavier it becomes. My thoughts are running a marathon through my heart, and the thought of trying again is exhausting. Please give me Your strength to feel again. I refuse to build my life in this valley. I know with You, all things are possible. So I will keep walking. Through the tears, the disappointments, the highs and lows, I'll keep walking. I'll rest in knowing that not everything that happens to me is good, but You can turn anything around for good and Your glory.

In Jesus' name

Amen

A Prayer to Get Out of Your Own Head

Hey God,

Sometimes, I will be in my own head, fighting for my life. I don't want to talk myself out of what You and I talk about. It seems that faith and doubt are at war for my heart, and I know that whichever voice I listen to will determine my path. Help me to see my life from Your point of view. I don't want to build my life based on pain, disappointments, or trauma. Give me Your peace that calms my mind and guides my heart. I know that if you call me to it, then You will see me through it. I don't need all the answers; I just need to follow you. So You be God, and I'll be obedient and meet you at the places that we talk about.

In Jesus's name

Amen

Heart Prayers

A Prayer to Not Fall in Lust

Hey God,

You know the desires of my heart, and You see the relationship that is in front of me. Open my eyes to see this relationship from Your point of view. I don't want to be intoxicated with lust and sober up with regret from my choices. Don't allow me to confuse lust with love and create a soul tie with a soul that is just passing by. The goal is to walk in love and not fall in lust. So, please remove anyone or anything that is not for me. You don't even have to explain.

In Jesus' name,

Amen.

A Prayer for Your Heart

Hey God,

Teach me how to guard my heart and not build a wall around it. Life has taught me how to remove it, and people have caused me to build a wall made of pain. I can't walk in love if I'm heartless. Teach me to build a gate instead so that I can let the right things and people in. Heal the areas that are broken and don't allow bitterness to become my vision. Teach me how to give and receive love and not be hindered from the pain of the past. I haven't met everyone in this life who will love me, and I don't want to reach the places that we talk about heartless. I will guard my heart and walk in love with people to the point they know it was You who taught me how to love.

In Jesus' name,

Amen.

A Prayer to Let Go and Grow

Hey God,

This thing that my heart is holding on to is killing me. I know that whenever You ask me to let go of something it's never to hurt me but to push me closer to You. You always know what I need, and I have learned that I can't build what You placed in my heart while holding on to things not meant for me. So, I release the things, people and pain that are holding me back from growing, and I will hold on to the things, people, and dreams that will strengthen my relationship with You as we walk to the places that we talk about.

In Jesus' name,

Amen.

A Prayer for Your New Normal

Hey God,

I guess this is the way things are going to be now. I would be lying if I said I saw things working out this way, but here we are. All I can do right now is give it all to You and trust that though I didn't see this coming, You did. Help me to see my life now from Your point of view. Guide me through the chaos of this to the places that we talk about. Help me to create something beautiful in this place. I might not be where I thought I would be at this point of my life, but as long as I'm with You, everything will work out.

In Jesus' name,

Amen.

A Prayer for When the Mind Replays What the Heart Can't Forget

Hey God,

I'm trying to move forward, but there are times when thoughts from what happened come out of nowhere and stop me in my path. It's like a gut punch to my heart, and it knocks the wind out of my hope. My memories quickly become nightmares. Help me to learn how to remember what happened but not relive it. I can't let what happened to me define my future. Yes, it happened, but I know You can make all things new-- even my future with You. Help me to step over what is tripping me up. Give me the strength to follow You and not my pain because I can't live my life back there. I know You can create a future so beautiful that it will heal the pain of the past. With You by my side, I will keep walking through what happened to the places that we talk about.

In Jesus' name,

Amen.

A Prayer for the Silent Battles

Hey God,

Each day within me, I fight a battle that no one knows about. I carry it well, but it's still heavy. These past few months I've had to wipe my own tears, catch my breath, pick myself up, and smile as I held it all together. The fight I'm in can feel lonely, but I can't confuse the feeling of loneliness with abandonment because through it all You have been there. I know that I'm not alone, and I know that I will have to fight some battles by myself. Give me the wisdom on how to handle the things that I don't talk about. Guide me to the right people and places that will help me through this. I know that You are with me and will turn my private battles into my public victories.

In Jesus' name,

Amen.

A Prayer to Forgive

Hey God,

You saw what happened. I am upset, hurt and angry. I am trying my best to not shutdown, but all I want is to get even. I don't want to grow bitter over time when the goal is to become more like You and not like those who hurt me. Give me strength to let this go. There is nothing that can fix what happened, and no answer can restore my peace-- only You can do that. I will forgive them, but I need You to help me heal. I can't allow this to infect my heart and change who I am and how I show up in future relationships. So, God, I forgive them. I will learn what I need to learn and become better and not bitter. Give me the wisdom to address what needs to be addressed, and I trust You to correct what needs to be corrected.

In Jesus' name,

Amen.

A Prayer for When You Face Rejection

Hey God,

You see what happened. If I'm honest, I go back and forth between being hurt and angry when I think about everything. The hardest part is that I may never get an answer to my questions of why and what did I do to deserve this, but I remind myself that You define my worth and not those who left or rejected me. When it got hard, You never left. I keep remembering that man's rejection is God's protection. Knowing that, I refuse to let rejection turn into bitterness and ruin the fruit of my future relationships. Heal my heart so it can be touched by people again. I refuse to allow one person's rejection to make me question Your acceptance.

In Jesus' name,

Amen.

A Prayer to Rest

Hey God,

I'm tired, and it's not the type of tiredness that a nap or a good night's sleep can fix. It's hard to rest when my thoughts never sleep. I need to quiet the waves of anxiety crashing against the peace of my heart. I've had a lot of questions about what happened with certain people and situations, but I realize that some answers will never bring me peace -- only more questions. So, I ask that You give me Your peace, which surpasses all my understanding and allows me to rest in knowing that all things will work out for good and Your glory.

In Jesus' name,

Amen.

A Prayer to Encourage Yourself

Hey God,

Recently, life has really been testing my mental, physical, and spiritual health. It's been harder than usual, and I really am trying. Help me to see myself the way that You see me. I know that if You called me to this place, then You will also see me through it. I know that I can do all things with You, including this. So, I will not let worry, fear, or anxiety talk me out of what You have for me. I trust You, and I will not stop walking to the places that we talk about.

In Jesus' name,

Amen.

A Prayer to Believe Again

Hey God,

Life has been rough, and I have wondered if You saw me. Everything that could go wrong went all the way wrong, and if I'm honest, I have struggled with my faith. Things just didn't make sense and all I could say is, "why me." I know that You said there would be tests, trials, and storms in this life, but I felt overwhelmed and abandoned. The pain of what happened made me drop my faith. Will You heal my heart from the pain of disappointment? It's hard to believe with a broken faith, but I will not allow my pain to talk me out of my faith. I know that not everything that happens to me is good, but You can turn anything around for my good and Your glory. I trust you, and I need You to help me pick up my faith and keep walking to the places we talked about.

In Jesus' name,

Amen.

A Prayer to Make Peace with Your Past

Hey God,

There are times when the thoughts of my past run a marathon through my mind. I constantly replay conversations and decisions and wonder if my life would be different if I had made different choices. I try to rest, but the thoughts of my past won't shut off. I know You said that You would make all things new, so help me to not allow what happened to me to determine who I become. I believe that You can create a future so beautiful that it heals the pain of the past. Help me to make right what I can and let go of what I cannot. I can't change the past, but I can learn from it. I will use those lessons to keep walking to the places that we talk about.

In Jesus' name,

Amen.

A Prayer for When Your Feelings Are Hurt

Hey God,

You saw what happened. I can't even lie; that really hurt my feelings. Though I know my feelings should not lead me, they are screaming right now, and it is hard to feel past them. So, in this moment, I ask that you help me to see past my feelings and not allow any seed of bitterness to grow from this situation. Please give me the wisdom on how to handle this best. Help me to see if I am taking something personally or if this is something that I need to address and resolve. Help me hear Your voice over my emotions because I don't want my emotions to talk me out of something that You provided for me.

In Jesus' name,

Amen.

A Prayer for When You're Triggered

Hey God,

You saw what just happened. That was like a gut punch to my peace. I thought I was better but that just reminded me of everything I'm trying to heal from. Help me to step over what used to trip me up. Give me the strength to follow You and not my pain. I refuse to go backwards. Yes, it happened to me, but it does not define or control me. I trust that with You all things are possible -- even creating a future so beautiful that it heals the pain of what happened. So, I will step over this trigger and keep walking towards You.

In Jesus' name,

Amen.

A Prayer for When Your Heart Is Grieving

Hey God,

My heart is broken. I don't understand everything, and it's hard to find the words to say right now. I go from smiling at the memories to crying from the pain of trying to forget. I try to be strong and move on, but it's hard to walk by faith with a broken heart. You said that You would give me beauty for ashes; so, I lay this down at your feet. Heal my heart so that I can feel again. Give me Your Peace, the kind that calms my thoughts and silences my fears. Even though I may not understand why this happened, I trust You to create a future so beautiful that it heals the pain of what happened. I know that not everything that happens to me is good, but I know that You can work anything out for my good and Your glory.

In Jesus' name,

Amen.

A Prayer for When You're Tempted to Quit

Hey God,

I have to be honest. This is a lot, and at times I go between staying strong and just walking away. I'm trying to run my race, but I feel like I'm running in quicksand. It seems that at every turn there is something or someone that just goes completely wrong. I know that I am strong but even the strongest man in the world can't hold up five pounds forever. I know that there will be trials in life, but it seems as if I am already sentenced before the trials even start. I'm fighting to not allow my trauma to become my vision. I know that You see me, and I trust that You can turn any mess into a miracle. Even though life is hard right now, I know where my help comes from. I trust that the fire of life will mold me to look like You and not what I have been through. You be God, and I will be obedient. I will keep walking to meet You at the place we talk about.

In Jesus' name,

Amen.

A Prayer for When You're Worried about Something

Hey God,

I'm going to be honest; I'm worried. The waves of life are constantly crashing against my peace, and I'm holding on to the hope that, "You work all things out for my good and Your glory." My thoughts are constantly running a marathon. My emotions are pulled and stretched, and my faith is being tested at every corner. You said that there would be trials in this life and that it would not be easy but to take heart. Well, I need Your heart because I can't allow worry to drown my faith. I want to go through this situation and not allow it to go through me. So, I come to You and lay down all the worry, anxiety, fears and burdens to pick up Your peace, joy, strength and heart. I can't do this alone; so, I will lean on You for You never fail.

In Jesus' name,

Amen.

A Prayer for When You're Angry

Hey God,

I know You saw that, right? They must think this is some kind of game. Why do people try me? I'm talking to You, because if I talk to my feelings, I'm going to flip more than tables, and we both know that I am still a work in progress. I know that I'm upset and need to address this, and I need You to help me do this the right way. Please give me the wisdom on what to say and the strength to not be petty, vindictive or disrespectful. Help me to see past my emotions and find a resolution in this situation, for You called me to be the salt of the earth and not a salty angry person.

In Jesus' name,

Amen.

A Prayer for Boundaries in A Relationship

Hey God,

Help me to remember that my job is not to solve everything for everyone that I love. It's hard because I want to save them, but my job is to love them, not to be their savior. I've realized that I ruin relationships when I'm the one saving people from lessons that You are trying to teach them. I was never meant to play the role of God in anyone's life. Help me to remember that boundaries protect my relationships; they don't restrict them. I have learned that You love people enough to let them learn a lesson, but You stick by them even in a mess. Thank You for showing me that my loyalty is not measured by my ability to fix everyone's problems. I can love people and have boundaries that protect our relationship and allow it to grow into something beautiful.

In Jesus' name,

Amen.

A Prayer for When You Make A Mistake

Hey God,

I messed up! That situation was my fault. I allowed my emotions to lead me, and I reacted. I messed up, and now I need to make it right. I have learned that not every bad thing that happens to me is an attack from the enemy, but some things are a result of my decisions. I refuse to allow my decisions to create a life that is in constant chaos, and I refuse to confuse condemnation with conviction. Though I made a mistake, I am not a mistake, and I know that You can help me fix any mistake. Guide me as I correct this situation. I will listen to Your voice as I apologize and make this right. May they hear my heart and may You heal theirs. Thank You for helping me make this right.

In Jesus' name,

Amen.

A Prayer for When You Feel Lonely

Hey God,

I feel alone right now. I know that You said You would never leave me, but some people have, even when they said that they wouldn't't. I don't want to confuse loneliness with solitude, for solitude brings peace, while loneliness brings isolation. People have hurt me, but I know the right people can heal me. I was created for relationships. So, I pray that You bring the right people into my life. Don't allow loneliness to make me "know" someone I should really say "no" to. Heal my heart because I can't walk in love with a broken heart. Even though I feel lonely right now, I will not allow it to dictate my worth. I refuse to settle in this valley when You are calling me towards people.

In Jesus' name,

Amen.

A Prayer for Closure

Hey God,

Help me to accept what happened. It's time to let go and move forward. I don't want to live in a fantasy of what could have been, should have been, or would have been. I want to walk by faith to the places that we talk about. You have taught me that, "it didn't work out" is not the same as, "it will never work out."

In Jesus' name,

Amen.

A Prayer for Overthinking

Hey God,

You see what's going on, and If I'm honest, I'm worried and overthinking this. I feel paralyzed to make a decision by my analysis of all that *could* happen. I'm having conversations with my emotions, and I'm creating nightmares. I'm trying to find a way to fix this, but every conclusion ends in disaster. I need You to help me find peace in the chaos of this situation because my thoughts are crashing against the peace of my heart, and it's hard to find rest. Help me to calm the wind and waves of my mind so that I may hear your voice. You never said there would not be storms in my life, but You did teach me that I could rest in a storm knowing that if You are with me, I can walk on what is trying to drown me.

In Jesus' name,

Amen.

A Prayer to Fight an Addiction

Hey God,

I'm fighting as hard as I can. This thing keeps trying to overtake me, but I won't let it. I have good and bad days, but I know that with Your help, I can be free from this. I will not allow this thing to overtake me and control my life. Help me to identify what this addiction is so that I can find healing. I don't want to depend on anything but You for my peace. Open my eyes to things or people that feed my addiction and help me to set up boundaries and remove stumbling blocks. I know that I can walk in freedom as I walk towards You.

In Jesus' name,

Amen.

A Prayer for the Times You Feel Petty

Hey God,

You saw that, right? They must think this is a game. Why do people try me? I'm talking to You right now because when I speak to my feelings, I will flip more than tables. And we both know that I am still a work in progress. I know I'm upset, but I need to address this, and I need to respond. I need you to help me do it in the right way. So please give me the wisdom on what to say and the strength not to be petty, vindictive, or disrespectful. Please help me see past my emotions and resolve this situation, for You called me to be the salt of the earth and not a salty person.

In Jesus' name

Amen.

A Prayer for When A Lot is Going On

Hey God,

There's a lot going on in my life right now. Some things are good. And some things are bad. I'm doing the best I can every day. I'm trying. I know You see everything. Please help me navigate this so I end up at the places we talk about. Give me the wisdom to handle tough decisions, the strength to keep walking, and Your peace that quiets the thoughts in my heart. I don't know how everything works out, but I trust that with You, everything will work out the way that it should.

In Jesus'

A Prayer of Acceptance

Hey God,

You saw everything that happened.

You saw my part, and You saw my heart. Please help me to accept whatever happens. You know the desires of my heart, and You also know what I need. So, if it is meant to be, then it will be. If not......
then I trust that You have something better. I know that you can work everything out for good and Your Glory. So, I will continue to work on myself for whatever may be or whoever is with me. And I will keep walking to the places that we talk about.

In Jesus' name

Amen

Jermiah 29:11 For I know the plans I have for you," says the Lord. "They are plans for good and not for disaster, to give you a future and a hope.

A Prayer to Move On

Hey God,

Well, it didn't work out how I thought it would. And here I stand, holding the pieces of "what could've been." I would be lying if I said I wasn't upset. But I don't like to think about it. Help me accept what happened and move forward. Just because this didn't work out doesn't mean that my life will not work out. So I will give You what's in my heart, and I will keep walking to the places that we talk about.

In Jesus' name

Amen

Steps to Letting Go:

1. Identify what is in your control and what is not.

2. Focus on what you can control.

3. Heal by releasing the memories and forgiving yourself and others. Give everything and everyone else to God in prayer.

4. Refocus and recenter your thoughts. Write down lessons you learned and write down what you want in the future.

5. Get to work on building the life that You and God talk about.

God can build a future so beautiful that it heals the pain of what happened…..

A Prayer to Declutter Your Heart

Hey God,

My heart is not a couch for anyone or anything to sit on, but I have a lot of things trying to sit on it. I'm tired of trying to make faith and trauma sit next to each other. I seem to carry everything well, but the truth is it's really heavy. Please help me to find peace by removing the things that don't serve me anymore. I've learned that only one thing can guide my heart, and I want that to be You. Not my past, my trauma, or my pain. I choose to walk by faith and step over my triggers, doubts, and insecurities as I walk to the places that we talk about.

In Jesus's name

Amen

A Prayer for When You're Tired

Hey God,

I'm tired. It's hard to walk by faith when I'm just trying to make it. My mind has been running a marathon through my heart. The journey has been long, and the places that we talked about seem so far away. I've heard that the strongest man in the world can't hold up 5 pounds forever because even the strongest of us get tired. Please give me Your strength. I refuse to build my life in this valley. I know that with You, all things are possible, even this. Give me Your peace that quiets the fears in my heart. And I will rest and keep walking. Through the tears, through the disappointments, the highs and the lows, I'll keep walking. I'll rest in You, for I know You have a way of working everything out for good and Your Glory. Even this situation I'm facing.

In Jesus's name

Amen

A Prayer to Feel Again

Hey God,

I'm trying to feel again, but it's hard at times. A lot has happened, and the thought of opening up my heart scares me. That last time was rough, and it led me to build a wall around my heart. I am glad I survived, but I feel like the cost was my heart. Help me to remove the wall I have placed around my heart. It was for protection, but I think it suffocates me. Teach me how to build a gate so that I can let the right things in my heart. I don't want to live a numb life. I want to feel. I want to embrace. I want to love. And I don't want to arrive at the places we talk about heartless.

In Jesus's name

Amen

A Prayer for Family Wounds

Hey God,

I thought that my family was my safe place, but the wounds I have tell me otherwise. The pain that I feel is indescribable. I don't feel safe with those who say they love me. I love them, but the experiences that I have had have damaged my heart. At times, I want to be loved and protected by those who call me their own. I've tried to fix it but learned that I can only love them. Help me navigate this in my heart and in my life. Please help me to heal from the wounds that are deep. I don't want my loved ones to suffer because of my family. I want a healthy relationship with my family. Bring people who can heal my family's wounds and change mindsets. I will always love them and want to see them live beautiful lives. Thank You for those who You have brought into my life to fill the void. And Thank You for being there through it all. I trust that you can heal this for me and my family.

In Jesus's name

Amen

A Prayer for Healing from the Trauma of Sexual

Hey God,

The struggle to feel love is hindered by the trauma of what happened. It wasn't my fault, but I feel as if my life has been a prison since I was violated. It's led to a broken heart that is guarded day and night. At night, it's hard to sleep because I never seem to wake up from the nightmare. Will You please heal my heart as only You can? I want to walk in love and not hide behind pain. I will need my heart, because I haven't met everyone in this life who will love me yet. May You bring people into my life who can show me true love's beauty. I know that people can hurt me, but I also know that the right people can heal me. I pray that You bring justice. I know that you can make all things new, even for me. I know that you can create a future so beautiful that it heals the pain of what happened.

In Jesus' name

Amen

Prayers for Life

A Prayer to Trust God with what You Can't Control

Hey God,

You see everything that I'm currently dealing with right now. There are some things that are just out of my control. I've tried everything that I know how to do, so now I give it all to You. Please give me Your peace that quiets my worries. I know that I can't control everything, and I don't know how everything will work out. But, I do know that even though not everything that happens to me is good in life, You can turn any situation around, even this one. So, You be God and I'll be obedient. No matter what it looks like, I trust You to work this out for my good and Your glory.

In Jesus' name,

Amen.

A Prayer to Try Again

Hey God,

Please give me the strength to try again. The memories of what happened before have tried to become my prison, and I feel stuck between a dream and a nightmare. Fear and faith are both at war for my heart, and I can't allow the fear of "what if" to become stronger than my faith that says "no matter what may come my way, with God anything is possible." I can't confuse the fact that it didn't work out the first time with, "it will never work out for me." I know the dream that You placed in my heart and where I am right now is not the place we talk about. So, I will get back up and try again, for I know that with You all things are possible.

In Jesus' name,

Amen.

A Prayer for Someone Who Is Sick

Hey God,

We need You. You see this situation, and You hear the diagnosis. It's a lot right now, and it's hard not to be worried. But, we walk by faith, and we know that anything is possible with You, even healing. So, we come to You and ask that you heal _____ as only You can. We trust that You guide the medical professionals with wisdom and empathy and that whatever they can't do, You will do. I pray that Your peace is the environment that we reside in no matter what happens. We know that regardless of what the report may be, our faith is rooted in knowing that all things work out for our good. May you provide healing and comfort for _____, and we will take this time to enjoy life with each other and make memories that will last a lifetime.

In Jesus' name,

Amen.

A Prayer for When You're Trying to Have Children

Hey God,

You see our hearts' desire to have children. One of the greatest honors of life is to love a child. We have tried, and it has been hard for many reasons. We have heard many reports. Some were good and some were not so good. It's been tough, but it hasn't changed our desire to have a child. So, we come to you and ask that You do the work that only You can do. Please heal any part of our body that needs healing, and if you are leading us to other options, please guide us towards what is best for us. We trust You, and our desire is to love and raise a child up who knows You. Heal the parts of our bodies, minds and hearts that have been impacted. We will need every part of us for the beauty of a child. You guide us, and we will follow You.

In Jesus' name,

Amen.

A Prayer for When You've Been Hurt by People in Church

Hey God,

My heart has been broken, and it came from those who said they love You. I'm trying to not let what they did to me overshadow all that You've done for me, but it's hard– especially when their love feels like hate. I feel bitterness hardening my heart towards church in general, and I don't want to be a part of any church that makes people feel like this. I need You to help me. Heal my heart and help me to separate them from You. I know that people can hurt me, but I also know that the right people can heal me. I refuse to let those who hurt me determine how I show up in my faith. Help me to confront hate but keep my heart. Help me not to punish everyone for the pain of a few. Please surround me with people that You have taught how to love, for I need You and the people that You place in my life to do the things You have placed in my heart.

In Jesus' name,

Amen.

A Prayer When You're Breaking Generational Cycles

Hey God,

This is tough. Nobody has really showed me how to live life like this before, and honestly nobody has really been in this position. I love my family and friends, but I don't want to repeat some of the same mistakes. I want to walk on the water, even if I'm the first one to step out of the boat. I will keep my eyes on You, and my faith will outwork any doubt, challenge or fear that may arise. I may not have the seen the blueprint, but I do know that You will provide the right opportunities and relationships to guide, push, mold and grow me. I know that with You all things are possible. I will keep my eyes on You and keep walking to the places we talk about.

In Jesus' name,

Amen.

A Prayer for Patience

Hey God,

Please develop in me the patience that I need to walk by faith to the places that we talk about. I don't want to rush into anything ahead of time. Don't allow me to confuse my faith with desperation. I don't want to be so desperate for something that I rush into something not meant for me. I don't want to open any doors or hearts that are not meant for me. If it's not from You then I don't want it, and if it's from You, it's worth waiting and preparing for. I always want to be led by You and not by my fear of being behind in life. If I'm ever moving too fast, please slow me down. Your correction is for my protection.

In Jesus' name,

Amen.

A Prayer for the In-between Seasons of Life

Hey God,

I'm not where I use to be, nor am I where I want to be, but I'm getting there. I'm holding on to the dream that You gave me despite my current reality. I know that if You call me to something, someone or someplace, then You will see me through it. Please give me the strength to stay the course that You have for me. I know that even though I can't see over some things in my way, I can always see You. If You're with me, I'm not lost or behind in life, but I'm right where I need to be. So, You be God, and I'll be faithful and will meet You at the places that we talk about.

In Jesus' name,

Amen.

A Prayer for a Good Hair Day

Hey God,

You know how much hair I have, so You know what's mine and what's borrowed. No matter what I may or may not have, help me to see myself through Your eyes and that I am not defined by my hair, no matter if I have a fresh cut, braids, fresh edges, curly, straight, or natural hair. Please let the curls fall the right way, let the edges lay and may my hair grow in all the right places. May it not frizz in the fire of today. No matter what this hair of mine does today, I pray that when people see me, they see Your heart shining through.

In Jesus' name,

Amen.

A Prayer for God's Provision

Hey God,

I trust You to provide everything I need in life. You see all that I need, and You're faithful to meet my needs. Please open every door in my life that needs to be opened and close every door that needs to be closed. Lead me to relationships that push me closer to You. Develop in me everything that I need to carry out the calling that You have for me. I've learned that You will do what I can't do, but You will not do what I can do. So, I will build with the vision and gifts that You've given me. Create in me a heart that is led by love and full of faith. If I need anything, I know that You will provide it for me. I've learned that You always provide where You guide. I'll look for You and Your provision as I continue to walk to the places that we talk about.

In Jesus name,

Amen.

A Prayer for When Someone Passes Away

Hey God,

I lost someone today. It hurts. I know that life is short and that we're not promised tomorrow, but I don't know if I was ready to say goodbye. My heart is grieving, and I'm holding on to the memories that we created. I pray that they are with You and in a better place. Help me to heal my heart and move forward in life. Help me to work through any guilt I may feel. There is so much I wish I could have told them, but I will live my life honoring them with the lessons and memories from our relationship.

In Jesus' name,

Amen.

A Prayer Before an Interview

Hey God,

I have a big day in front of me.

I have worked really hard and prepared for this day. I feel excited, anxious, confident, and nervous all at the same time. I know that what You have for me is for me. I pray that I am prepared to handle the opportunity in front of me. Help me to communicate my heart and wisdom for this opportunity. If this is not for me, close the door. If it's not for me, then I know You have something better. I trust You to open every door that needs to be opened in my life. Thank You!

In Jesus' name,

Amen.

A Prayer Before a Test

Hey God,

I have a big test today. I'm nervous because I want to pass this test and do well. Help me to keep my mind alert and my memory sharp. If there are distractions, please remove them. Help me to recall and apply everything that is needed. I will not let anxiety or stress cloud my concentration. I know that I can do all things through Christ and that includes passing this test.

In Jesus' name,

Amen.

A Prayer to Resist Temptation

Hey God,

You see this thing that is coming after me. I am just minding my business, but the enemy is trying to trip me up. I will not fall for the traps of the enemy. I have come too far to throw away everything for nothing. Help me to be strong and resist. I know that if Jesus was tempted, I surely will be tempted. But, Jesus has shown me the way, and I choose to walk in purpose and not fall into temptation. We have too much to accomplish, and I want to use my faith to accomplish the dream You have placed in my heart instead of getting me out of trouble that I choose.

In Jesus name,

Amen.

A Prayer for When You're Trying to Lose Weight

Hey God,

Why does food taste so good?!

My health is important, but I can't walk by faith if I can't even walk up a flight of stairs. I don't want to have to use my faith for healing because of a lack of discipline. Please give me the strength to change my mindset towards healthy eating. Is there an anointing for working out? If not, I will be disciplined to show up every day. I want to be fit spiritually and physically. I want to wear the whole armor of God and my favorite jeans. I don't want to stop walking by faith because I can't physically keep up with where you are taking me. Can You please do me one favor? Please make cookies and cake taste like bitter onions.... Thank You.

In Jesus' name,

Amen.

A Prayer for Healing

Hey God,

You see all that I am dealing with right now-- physically, emotionally, and spiritually. I'm literally fighting for my health. I come to You for healing with my faith based on Jesus and Your word. With my body in pain and my emotions all over the place, I stand on Your truth and believe You for my healing. Give me the strength to stand strong, Your peace that quiets my worries, and the wisdom on what to do. I know that You have blessed us with doctors and medicine, and I pray that You guide them during this time. If there is anything that natural medicine cannot heal, I know that You can. I know that not everything that happens to me in life is good, but I know that You can work everything out for my good and Your glory. I know that healing is a journey, and I'm glad that You're walking with me, for I know that all things are possible with God.

In Jesus' name,

Amen.

A Prayer for The First Day of a New Season

Hey God,

The day is finally here. I'm excited and nervous but hopeful. As I walk into this new season, I pray that You guide my steps. I pray that You give me wisdom in this new season to make decisions that bring me closer to You. Please open every door that needs to be opened and close every door that needs to be closed. Equip me with what I need for whatever this season may bring. Help me recognize the people You are bringing into my life in this new season, and help me accept the relationships that ended in the last season. No matter what this new season may bring, I know You are with me.

In Jesus' name,

Amen.

A Prayer for When It's Hard to Get out of Bed

Hey God,

As I lay here, it feels like the weight of my world is holding me down. I feel covered in anxiety, and it's hard to see the bright side of anything right now. If I'm honest, I would rather just stay here and hope tomorrow is better. My faith and my doubt are wrestling for control of my heart, and I know that in order to walk by faith, I have to get up to walk. Please give me strength. Yes, I have had some hard days, hard relationships, and disappointments, but I know with You, all things are possible. I know that You can create a future so beautiful that it heals the pain of the past. So, I'm getting up and walking by faith today. I know it will not be perfect, but with You, I know that everything will work out. Please give me the peace that calms my understanding. Today might not be perfect, but it will be beautiful.

In Jesus' name,

Amen.

A Prayer for When You Have a Bad Day

Hey God,

Well, today was pretty bad. Everything that could go wrong went all the way wrong. Even when I tried to fix things, they just became worse. I knew that I would have bad days, but I can't allow this bad day to have me. I have survived bad days before, and I know this, too, shall pass. **I will not allow my emotions to lead me to make a decision that will last longer than this day.** I have learned that bad days don't last forever, and even good times seem to have a curfew. But, no matter what, You are with me. So, help me see beyond today, and I will do what I can to make the best of what has happened.

In Jesus' name,

Amen.

A Prayer While You Wait on God

Hey God,

I'm holding on to the word that You gave me, but it's hard when you're in the middle of walking from what was spoken to what will be. If I'm honest, where I am standing looks nothing like what we talked about, and I question if I made a wrong turn at some point. But, I know that If You called me to it, You will see me through it. Even though I'm in the middle of an unfamiliar place, I am surrounded by faith. Give me the wisdom to see this from Your point of view. I will not allow the wait to make me confuse delay with denial. I know that You are preparing me and the place that You have shown me, and I don't want to walk into any place that I am not prepared for. You be God, and I will be obedient as I keep walking. I know with You the outcome is always worth the wait.

In Jesus' name,

Amen.

A Prayer to Unlearn What No Longer Serves You

Hey God,

I have been through a lot in my life, and I have learned how to take care of myself. But, I have realized that some things I have learned help me survive but not live. I don't want to be so guarded in my life that I wall off my heart and show up to new relationships heartless. I can't poison my faith with the pain of my disappointments. Please help me to unlearn what is no longer good for me. I don't just want to survive; I want to live. I don't want to just dream about things; I want to walk on the path of the impossible towards those dreams. I don't want to push people away because of pain and call it discernment. Please help me unlearn what no longer serves me and create a clean heart in me as I keep walking to the places that we talk about.

In Jesus' Name

Amen

A Prayer to Not Become Attached to Things Not For You

Hey God,

Please help me to say no to something that may look good at the moment but will cause chaos in the future. If it's not for me and not from You, then I don't want it or need it. I trust You and will wait for what you have for me. Develop in me all that I need to walk into the places, relationships, and opportunities that You have for me. I know that Your correction is for my protection. And I want my choices to create memories with what You have for me and not messes that we have to clean up.

In Jesus' name

Amen

A Prayer for Restoration

Hey God,

I've survived a lot of stuff in my life, but I've also lost a lot just trying to survive some things. I'm trusting You to restore everything that was lost, stolen, or destroyed in my life. Some things were my fault, and some things were out of my control. But I refuse to believe the lie that restoration is not for me when scripture says that You can make all things new. I know that You can create a future so beautiful that it heals the pain of the past. So, I trust You, and I will keep walking to the places we talk about.

In Jesus' name

Amen

A Prayer to Pivot

Hey God,

Please help me to know when it's time to move in a different direction. I don't want to hang on to something that You're removing, and I don't want to be in a place that is no longer meant for me. I want to be led by You. Please give me the wisdom to know what to pick up and what to put down. Please open up every door in my life that needs to be opened and close every door that needs to be closed. I trust You, and I want what You have for me. Even if I don't understand everything., I know what You have for me is good and leading me to the places that we talk about.

In Jesus' name

Amen

A Prayer Before You Have a Tough Conversation

Hey God,

I have to have a tough conversation with _____.
This conversation is necessary, and it is time. I want to communicate in a way that brings peace to this situation. Please help me not to be led by my emotions in this conversation. Help me to hear the truth that I need to hear. I pray that you prepare the heart of _____ to receive for this conversation. I know that honesty is kind, but it can be painful. I want to build a healthy relationship and know that tough conversations are where healthy relationships are built.

In Jesus' name

Amen

EASTER Day Prayer

Hey God,

Thank You for knowing everything about me and still choosing me, loving me, and redeeming me. Thank You for showing me the definition of true love through Jesus. He overcame betrayal, politics, corrupt religious systems, lies, trauma, heartbreak, death, and the grave, and He conquered it all and rose again. Thank You for everything. I would not be here without You. I cannot ever pay You back, but I can give You my life, pick up my cross, and follow You to the places that we talk about.

In Jesus' name

Amen

Christmas Day Prayer

Hey God,

This Christmas, I just want to tell You………..Thank You. Life has not always gone according to plan. People came into my life, and people have left my life. My heart smiled, and my heart broke. I have seen the mountaintop, and I have lived in the valley. I have walked through nightmares to get to the places that we talk about. And I have made some good decisions, and I have made some bad decisions. But choosing to follow You has been the best decision of my life. No matter who left, You always stayed. When I messed up, You helped me clean it up. When I was at my lowest, You walked with me. Thank You for knowing everything about me and still choosing me, pushing me, correcting me, believing me, and loving me. This Christmas, I know I could never pay You back, but this Christmas, I am giving You my heart. And I will live a life where when people see me, they don't see me, but they see You shining through..

In Jesus' name

Amen

Mother's Day Prayer

Hey God,

For every Mom.

For every soon-to-be Mom.

For the one filling the role of Mom.

We Thank You. The love of a mother is powerful. Their love teaches us what it means to love someone more than ourselves. They're our cheerleaders, supporters, safe places, miracle workers, prayer warriors, doctors, truth-tellers, and friends. Please give them strength and wisdom as they walk with us through life. May You give them rest. For those mothers who may have experienced loss, I pray that You provide them with comfort as only You can. For the Mom's who are sick, I pray that You heal them as only You can. I pray that all those who fill the role of Mom and for their sacrifice of love. May all mothers know they are loved and not alone. And May their hair always be on point, their edges laid, their curls popping, their smiles full of life, and hearts filled with love, peace, and beautiful memories.

In Jesus' name

Amen

A Prayer for Fathers

Hey God,

For Every Father

For every soon-to-be Father

For every person that we call "Dad."

Thank You for them. They have taught us so many beautiful lessons. They have taught us how to believe in ourselves through their love and belief in us. They have taught us how to be strong and do what is right even when it is not easy. They have taught us the beauty of hard work and sacrifice. They have loved us through their actions. Please let every Father know that they are not alone in the role that You have given them. Continue to provide them with the strength to lead us to the places that You have for us. Please provide them with the wisdom to help guide us through life. And give them Your heart to love us through the tough times. Thank You for Your gift of love through Fathers.

In Jesus' Name

Amen.

Affirmations

Affirmations to Start Your Day

Today is a gift, and I will not take it for granted.

I am loved and worthy of love.

I will leave everyone I come in contact with today better than I found them.

No matter what happens today, I will walk by faith.

My faith will outwork my doubt.

I have feelings, but they do not have me.

I forgive those who have hurt me.

When people see me today, they will see God shining through.

God supplies all of my needs, and I will use what He gives me to build the vision that You have placed in my heart.

I will not allow fear, anxiety, or worry to consume me. No matter what happens, God can work everything out for my good and His Glory.

Nighttime Affirmations

Nighttime can be a peaceful time of dreams and rest, or it can be a nightmare as every thought and emotion you outran all day catches up with you. One thing that has helped me during this time is remembering that I can only control what I can, and no matter what happens, God and I will walk through the good, bad, and ugly together.

Repeat these until you can see them in your heart.

1. It didn't work out is not the same as it will never work out for me. So, I will keep working.

2. Nothing is too hard for God. I will rest in knowing that with God, all things are possible.

3. Even though everything that happened to me is not good, God can turn anything around for good and His glory.

4. I'm not behind, for God redeems time.

5. I will use my faith to outwork my worries. Instead of dwelling on the problem, I will dwell on what God told me, what I can do, and leave the rest in God's hands.

6. I'm not alone, for God never leaves me.

7. I'm worthy of love.

Growth Prayers

God, I forgive them.

God, don't let me remain in the same place this time next year.

God, please remove whatever or whoever is keeping me from growing in You and add whatever or whoever pushes me closer to You.

God, teach me how to love and receive love.

God, make me the answer to a problem.

God, correct me if I'm wrong and turn me around if I'm going the wrong way.

God, help me to see people through your eyes and not my insecurities, pain, or trauma.

In Jesus name,

Amen.

Faith Prayers

God, even when I can't see you working, I believe that You're working. So, I will keep working.

God, I will not quit. If You called me to it, I know You will see me through it.

God, I believe the faith in my heart more than the doubt in my head.

God, please teach me how to walk on what is trying to drown me.

God, I will place my rock of obedience in my slingshot of worship and kill the giants before me.

God, help me to not allow my disappointments to talk me out of my faith.

In Jesus' name

Amen.

What are you believing God for in this season of your life?

Heart Prayers

God, please keep my heart soft and with wisdom and boundaries.

God, please teach me how to go through things in life and become better and not bitter, tough, or mean.

God, please teach me how to step over my triggers and keep walking to the places that we talk about.

God, please teach me how to remain pure in my heart and not tainted by the world. I want to see You. I don't want to gain the world and arrive at the places we talk about heartless.

God, please teach me how to guard my heart and not build a wall around it.

In Jesus' name,

Amen.

Relationship Prayers

God, please teach me how to love people so well that they know I learned how to love from You.

God, show me the purpose of each relationship in my life.

God, teach me how to work through conflict in a relationship. Please don't allow me to throw away something that needs to be fixed or hang on to something that I need to let go.

God, teach me who to "know" in life and who to "no" in life.

God, I pray that love is the theme of my relationships.

God, I pray that my relationship grows healthier and not toxic over time.

In Jesus' name,

Amen.

Life Prayers

God, give me the strength and wisdom to handle whatever happens to me in this life.

God, I trust You. I can't always see You working, but I trust that You are working, So I will keep working.

God, don't allow the disappointments of my life talk me out of the faith in my heart.

God, keep me balanced. May a win never go to my heart, and may a loss never infect my heart.

God, may I live in such a way that when people see me, they actually see You shining through.

God, please teach me who to "know' in life and who to "no" in life.

In Jesus' name

Amen

I hope that these prayers help you continue to walk to the places that you and God talk about. Remember this, God knows everything about you, and He still loves you, believes in you and is for you.

Keep Walking

Keep the Faith

Keep Loving

Keep Believing

I can't wait to hear about the places that you go and stories you create as You walk with God.

- Solomon

Hey God Journal

Use the following pages to journal your walk with God. Use it to write your own prayers, reflect on important moments, or write down your life lessons.

Hey God

Hey God

Hey God

Hey God

Hey God

_____
_____
_____
_____
_____
_____
_____
_____
_____
_____
_____
_____
_____
_____
_____
_____
_____
_____
_____
_____
_____
_____
_____
_____
_____
_____
_____
_____

Hey God

Hey God

(lined page for writing)

Hey God

Hey God

167

Hey God

Hey God

Hey God

_____
_____
_____
_____
_____
_____
_____
_____
_____
_____
_____
_____
_____
_____
_____
_____
_____
_____
_____
_____
_____
_____
_____
_____
_____
_____

Hey God

Hey God

Hey God

Hey God

Hey God

Hey God

_____

_____

_____

_____

_____

_____

_____

_____

_____

_____

_____

_____

_____

_____

_____

_____

_____

_____

_____

_____

_____

_____

_____

_____

_____

_____

_____

_____

Hey God

Hey God

Hey God

_____

_____

_____

_____

_____

_____

_____

_____

_____

_____

_____

_____

_____

_____

_____

_____

_____

_____

_____

_____

_____

_____

_____

_____

_____

_____

_____

_____

_____

_____

_____

_____

_____

_____

_____

_____

Hey God

Hey God

_____

_____

_____

_____

_____

_____

_____

_____

_____

_____

_____

_____

_____

_____

_____

_____

_____

_____

_____

_____

_____

_____

_____

_____

_____

_____

_____

_____

_____

181

Hey God

Hey God

Hey God

Hey God

_____
_____
_____
_____
_____
_____
_____
_____
_____
_____
_____
_____
_____
_____
_____
_____
_____
_____
_____
_____
_____
_____
_____
_____
_____
_____
_____

Hey God

Hey God

Hey God